THE CREATOR OF ALL THE COSMIC IAM

and other collected works

By Josiah Osuagwu - The Cosmic Son
and Anthony Torres
Compiled and annotated by
Anthony Torres

THE CREATOR OF ALL
THE COSMIC IAM
and other collected works

This material is the collected works of an ancient wise soul and teacher of Cosmic consciousness, named Josiah Osuagwu, The Cosmic Son. This work contains additions by his student Anthony Torres. These pages include direct revelation and knowledge Josiah received from The Creator, titled 'The Cosmic IAM.' As well, within this collection is: 'Meditation system for reuniting with The Creator of All,' 'Proclamation & Prayer to The Creator for Guidance,' and other assorted writings on Cosmic Consciousness and Conscious Cosmic Citizenship by Josiah Osuagwu.

Written by Josiah Osuagwu

Compiled and annotated by Anthony Torres

Published by New Aeon Solutions Publishing

The Creator of All - The Cosmic IAM by Josiah Osuagwu
Produced by Anthony Torres
Published by New Aeon Solutions

NEW AEON SOLUTIONS
—— PUBLISHING ——

3151 Airway Ave., Suite L1, Costa Mesa, CA, 92626
For permissions, contact: anthony@gold-encompass.com

Cover by Oladimeji Alaka
Edited by Hill Hugh

For information about special discounts available for bulk
purchases, sales promotions, fund-raising, and educational needs,
please contact New Aeon Solutions Publishing Company sales at:
anthony@gold-encompass.com

Profits from this book
go to charities for homeless women and single mothers

First Edition

Dedicated to The Creator of All and Josiah Oswuagwu

Gratitude and special acknowledgments to all of Josiah's family, students, and friends who extended a helping hand in caretaking and providing earthly assistance to him while he was here.

A special appreciation to Adama Alaji for all that she did for Josiah and for her dedication to the furthering and teaching of Conscious Cosmic Citizenship and Josiah's teachings.

Contents

Preface

The collective human mind, in large, has been built upon the central premise that we are temporal-flesh beings, living in a world of form, and that our Source, God The Creator is separate from us, existing *out there* somewhere. Thusly, throughout history, utilizing allegory, myths, rituals, and belief systems, religions and philosophical movements have become the surrogates and self-purported necessary bridges to The Creator of All. The intention of this work is to help people in consciously reestablishing their coherent connection with The Creator of All, in a personal one-in-one, unified, familial way.

This manuscript is intended to help teach *Reality*, *Relationship* and *Responsibility*, rather than belief. *Reality* being the waking up to the knowing and experience of what we truly are as undying immortal Spirit Mind. Your

Being and very life, as well as All of existence, is within, and of the Mind-Body of The Creator of All. In the knowing of this is the establishing of your continuation in existence without death.

Relationship being that we share an innermost essence with each other and our Mother-Father Creator. We have been created in, and together forever share, a Love that has no opposites and no ending. We are all the purposefully created and beloved Child of God.

Responsibility being the knowing and doing of your True-Will and function in tune with the Whole Cosmic, as prescribed by The Creator – instead of an autonomous self-determined free-will operating under the guise of separation and the illusions of the temporal-self.

Introduction

It is my humble and sincere honor to bring this collection of works by Josiah Osuagwu, The Cosmic Son, to you. My name is Anthony Torres. I have been a student of Sons since 1997. Much of the material presented here are Josiah's teachings, which he produced before I met him. The documents titled "Petition, Proclamation & Prayer to The Creator for Guidance," and "The Cosmic IAM Meditation System" are both teachings he created and shared with me in 1997 and 2002.

Although his work being of the highest significance, Son was not someone who sought after worldly acknowledgment or exposure. I was always curious why his teachings had not been made public or compiled into book form by any of his past students. After his passing a few years back, from the respect and reverence in my heart, I felt the pull to publish his teachings, for everyone they may help.

I originally heard about Son through a friend of mine who met him while visiting a shop called Mother Earth's Adornments in Little Five Points, Atlanta, Georgia, which one of Son's students, Adama, owned at the time.

I was 17 years old the first time I met Son. At the time I was a lost young man on a dark path. Regardless of this, he lovingly shared his wisdom of The Creator of All and existence with me. Son not only helped shape my understanding of Self, existence, and The Creator, but he also helped save my soul. Son was not just a mentor and teacher to me; he was like a spiritual father.

Upon visiting him, I saw was a healthy-looking older man, standing about 5 foot 7. He exuded wisdom. He had white Einstein-like hair, and eyes that contained a sparkle of endless love. He emanated a serenity that I had never felt before: the energy of sincere peace, delivered through a gentle smile. His energy felt ancient. I knew I was standing in the presence of a soul of greatness and mastery. Son spoke in clear English with an endearing African accent and had a very developed intelligent vocabulary.

Son introduced himself with, *Greetings I am Son*, then explained about his work in teaching Cosmic Consciousness, Cosmic Law, and The Creator of All. He referred to The Creator as The Cosmic IAM. He began sharing and explaining a few things to me. While doing so, he pulled out a piece of light blue paper and write out a statement of intention, which was an appeal of sorts, to The Creator for me to declare. At that time of my life, I couldn't yet fully comprehend the magnitude of his words. I would grow to realize this moment was the first step to helping me upon my journey to healing and eventually onto the path of wisdom and reunion with The Creator of All. I have included the document in mention in Chapter 2: "Proclamation & Prayer to The Creator of All."

As a teen, I would meet with Son on multiple occasions. Between 19 and 23 years old, I did not see Son at all. During this time, I made many necessary life changes, setting me on the spiritual path, and leaving behind my dark past.

At 23 years old, I reconnected with Son and offered to have him come live with me and take over his caretaking responsibilities, while he did his work. Once arranged, we proceeded forward and lived together for a few years in the early-to-mid 2000s.

Our time living together was tremendous. It was an honor to both be of assistance to and learn from him. Son would spend most of his time working in the other dimensions, in a conscious, multi-located manner, guided wherever The Creator deemed necessary for teaching or expressing corrections to other aspects of creation in existence. When he wasn't working in this capacity, he would share many things with me and teach me about The Creator of All, existence, and Cosmic consciousness.

One of the things Son shared with me was the internal steps, which were unearthed from within him in 1977 and 1978, which facilitated his process of meeting The Creator of All. This meditation system is found in Chapter 10, "The Cosmic IAM Meditation System."

Before he wrote out the steps on paper, I listened to him explain them. As he did his body looked as if it was illuminating like a body-sized candle flame of light surrounding him. It was one of the most astonishing visual experiences of my entire life.

Josiah was a master and someone who maintained an ever-present focus toward his duty and prescribed responsibilities from The Creator. He was unyieldingly devoted to doing the work of The Creator of All and teaching the knowledge of The Creator and the precepts of Cosmic Consciousness and Conscious Cosmic Citizenship, on earth and beyond. He was someone with a work ethic like I have never seen before. There were times while Son was living with me that he would work twenty hours or more a day, for days in a row. He was highly focused on and never yielded from the core message of his teachings: The knowing and doing of The Creator's Will, rather than living life from the singular self-determination of the temporal-separate-self.

Son always emphasized the importance of using meditation for communicative listening to The Creator, for asking and knowing The Creator's position and point of view from a situation-by-situation, decision-by-decision basis for one's life.

He would often express to me the importance of being mindful of who to or not to have sexual relations with. He taught me that The Creator had designed and set within its will specific partners for each person and that not everyone was energetically designed for each other. He explained how important it is to use internal communication with The Creator for guidance in knowing who to, or not to engage in sexual intimacy with. He explained that each woman on the earth was a highly sensitive Cosmic center and cell of The Creator's Cosmic reproductive system. This Cosmic reproductive system being the faculty of creation which births existences, dimensions, and worlds into being. When a woman has sex with a man who is not in alignment with The Creator's design and Will for her, it creates an energetic decline effect and dims one's soul Light. This which ripples into the macrocosmic birthing faculties of existence. This aspect of his teachings was very instrumental in the greater cultivation of my reverence toward women and my mindfulness around sexual intimacy.

Son taught that Earth is a center point for many dimensions and universes. And that it was supposed to be governed by women who were in Light/conscious union with The Creator. He explained that this earth was originally intended to be a symposium for teaching souls the process for attaining the Wisdom of deliberate conscious communication with The Creator of All, for living in The Creator's will versus self-determination.

When I asked him about his stance on the use of plant medicines or substances, such as psychedelics, to attain enlightenment or be on a spiritual path, his exact words were, "You do not need to use those things when you have the opportunity to learn from The Creator directly."

Son often expressed a discerning caution about organizations of this world, who place books, philosophy, holy figures, or religious practices above direct conscious connection and communication with The Creator of All. He was clear about the instruction that "in the air, in the water, on the earth, in the universe, and/or on any various dimensions, to never worship or bow to any other creation or organization of creation above or before The Creator of All."

As I've moved through life after my time with Son, his lessons, knowledge, and initiations have continued to ripple through me with a constant influence on my unfolding. In that, my gratitude is beyond measure and expression. The production of this book is the closest way I know to show my appreciation.

Blessings! Enjoy!

Chapter 1

The Journey of Josiah
Osuagwu - The Cosmic Son

Josiah Osuagwu was born in February 1935 in the village of Umunachi-Obowo, Nigeria. Josiah was prophesied as a spiritual leader by his tribe in Nigeria before his birth. In 1961, he arrived in the United States, where he studied at Indiana State College, graduating in 1964, later going on to attend an undergraduate program at the University of Pittsburgh.

Josiah's spiritual journey began in 1966 after graduating from college. Rather than following a worldly career, he instead dedicated his life to the pursuits of spiritual knowledge and wisdom, with the central desire to know and discover The Creator of All.

It would be during 1977-78 that he would be guided into revelation, knowledge, and wisdom of The Creator of All. Josiah arrived at this through a set of internal steps, which he said were revealed within him. In this, his consciousness merged with and was guided by the Light of existence, through the sequential levels, planes, and dimensions of manifest creation, back to The Creator of All, unto Its unmanifest form and Presence.

This experience of reunion and revelation with The Creator in 1977/78 inspired Josiah's writing of 'The Cosmic IAM,' found in Chapter 9 - which is the centerpiece and foundational purpose of this book. The purpose of 'The Cosmic IAM' is to serve as an ode to The Creator of All and a first-hand testament of revelation, explaining the nature of The Creator of All.

He would be given the name The Cosmic Son, or Son, and go on to begin his ministry of Cosmic consciousness. Josiah would refer to The Creator of All as 'The Cosmic IAM.' It was during this time that Josiah taught students on the physical plane for more than ten years. After this, he began his work primarily on the non-physical sides of existence, wherever The Creator guided him to go. Through what he called his 'Destiny body,' his consciousness would be transported to various places where he would spend his days teaching the laws and will of The Creator of All to various parts of creation that were out of alignment with The Creator's will.

Josiah often spoke of a Cosmic court system, which he co-created, called the 'Tribunal of the Whole,' also known as the 'Cosmic Court of Appeal.' This was a court system on the higher dimensions of existence, which seats the ancestors of existence, designed to hold beings and groupings of beings accountable for defaulting against The Creator and Cosmic law.

Josiah spent much of the later years of his work producing motions or laws into existence to be passed by The Tribunal of The Whole and The Creator. These consisted of Cosmic principles, revealed to him by The Creator, for creation to abide by. The purpose of this was to support the healing and realignment of all of creation with the wisdom of The Creator's Will and plan for existence. This he referred to as "Cosmic Destiny."

Josiah Osuagwu – The Cosmic Son, lived in the Atlanta, Georgia area until the age of 83, where he then moved on from natural causes.

Chapter 2

~~~⚬~~~

Proclamation & Prayer to
The Creator of All

The following is a declaration and request to The Creator of All for guidance in obtaining the knowledge and experience of immortal Self, and Wisdom of one's God-prescribed Purpose. When spoken with sincerity, readiness, and surrender, these words initiate the path of the awakening and experience of one's Organic Reality as immortal Spirit and union with The Creator.

This request is to help one avoid a life of spiritual sleep and purposeless aimless wanderings through this world of flesh-identification, self-determining, and the illusion of separation from The Creator.

May you read these words intently and solemnly, from within your heart of hearts. Be allowing, be patient, and be sincere with these words, and they will change what you understand as life, eternally.

* O' Creator of All that is All, please place me in your Absolute and Eternal Light, Wisdom, Knowledge, Truth, and Justice

* I am an inherent part of your Presence and Purpose, O' Creator of All

* Grant me to know who and why I am what I am

* Please teach me Cosmic destiny and Cosmic citizenship

* I accept the blessings of All of your Cosmic Presence and Existence

* I accept the peace which is your pleasure within me

* I claim The Creator that is All for my worship

Chapter 3

~~~~~~~~~

Where the People have Lost their Purpose

Part 1

Nations and races who have lost their inherent and original Creator-prescribed purpose have also lost their succinct and natural destiny.

When and where people have lost their purpose, every form of their achievement, no matter how high, fails to give rise to the reward of doing one's organic destiny.

The design for human residency of the earth is completely purposeful and scheduled.

The loss of organic purpose is the real downfall of goddesses and gods, the woe of angels and humans, and the banishment of elemental species.

There are no more confused and unprogressive peoples and nations than there are those who have lost their mandated global and local natural purpose prescribed by their Creator.

There are no more idle and unemployed nations and races than those who have lost their purpose or who now labor for mistaken and incorrect purposes.

Who are not humiliated nor humbled by glimpses and realizations of the inherent misfortune in losing one's purpose?

Beware then, of the nations and folks which have lost their purpose, motto, and destiny. Many such races, nations, and personalities give the world reason to doubt that there is a Law of the Whole or an All-Administering Intelligence. They are the reasons why so many are misled into "believing" there is NO Creator of ALL, or that the Cosmic has no faithful order and justice.

We are to realize that everyone who was nailed upon the cross for righteousness' sake, everyone who was thrown into the lion's den, and everyone who was drawn into popular or unpopular wars, suffered as such on account of peoples and nations who have lost their purpose.

We must beware then of the progress, greatness, and grandeur of the races that have lost their purpose. Theirs is the progress of abdication, the grandeur of unsuspected woes, and the greatness of bluff and insecurity.

If by chance you come in contact with or catch a glimpse of knowing of their genuine destiny, please speak faithfully and truthfully, even cautiously, unto them who have lost their purpose: they are as a people who lost everything, or otherwise, a people who have nothing whatsoever to lose.

Please help The Creator to help them – but beware of how you listen to them. For this truism shall and will always prevail: It is far better to listen to their Creator than to listen to the people who have lost their purpose!

Within their natural destiny and purpose, a people will recover their lost mind. But, within their loss of purpose, just about everything is lost... body, mind, soul, and Light.

A nation or peoples who have lost their organic earth residence purpose have also lost their universal and Cosmic purpose. While theirs becomes a life of inorganic happenstances and arbitrary discretions, they must be considered "lucky" if they still have some idols as their Creator, or some doctrines as their conscious constitutional guiding light.

There are no limits to the transgressions that are potentially possible to a people who have lost their purpose. Also, just about anything can happen to them. You see, folks who have lost their Creator-Bestowed-Purpose: peoples, nations, or races who are no longer in contact with inherent destiny, live a life of continuous trespasses, even while they seem to be doing as well as those who are in touch with their own genuine destiny.

Again, you see, it's not a matter of mechanically doing things efficiently, rather, it's a matter of doing righteously that which is applicable as genuine Creator-prescribed destiny.

All true purpose is All destiny comprehending.

Part 2

In the torrent of the ocean of infinite and eternal events in the Cosmic, The Creator, The Ever-present Cosmic Supreme Being and All-Knowing Intelligence, uses purpose to maintain the float and ambience of things.

Cosmic Law, the law of the Supreme and Absolute entirety of Cosmic Omnipresence of being, uses purpose to keep folks in right alignment.

In this ocean, those who have lost their purpose toss about in tempestuous lack of direction in indefinite crests, deeps, and furors of unprofitable evolutionary experiences. Although their journeys have been generally arduous and long, they who have lost their purpose have nowhere to arrive… they have broken with destiny.

How can you console them in their misfortune? How can you assist them in regaining their mandatory purposes? What are people who have lost their purpose living and hoping for?

What use is the geopolitics of East and West; spirit and scripture; race and prejudice; affluence and want, or death and immortality, where and when the people have lost their Creator-prescribed purpose?

What value is freedom, liberty, and love unto a people who have lost their purpose?

By their listening to one another instead of listening to their Creator, it is a constant funerary in the death-rituals of purposeless existence.

Of this fact, you need to note seriously: There are no people who have lost their true purpose, who have not also forgotten the original Source of their lost purposes, or who have not broken with the umbilical line and root unto the aboriginal Source and Cause.

Now, how can you reassure, or even save a people who have lost their purpose? How can one assist them without increasing their imperilment? You must, of all things, listen to their Creator – not to them! By doing so, you are enabled to monitor their organic destiny and natural talent according to the highest applicable formula of their

Creator for them. You can reconnect them with their lost Light of Supreme Intelligence and guiding Wisdom, instead of reconnecting them with religious historical events and experiences which make no sense in helping them out of their imperilment – which might impel them to repeat the bitter end of olden times.

Then, that you know of communication with The Creator, you must think for them in their thoughtlessness, and do for them their undone chores, until that point and place where they can join you without jeopardy to both yourself and them.

Again, you must monitor their organic destiny and natural talents, not their social ideals and current works. You must uncompromisingly and resolutely keep pointing them to their Original Source and Cause of Purpose: The Creator of All. If you happen to be unable to re-identify and re-affirm them with their Original Source and Cause of Purpose, you are yourself, as a person whose cause, if not purpose, is already lost.

This you must realize without fail: People who have lost their purpose are constitutionally a selfish people. Their visions and goals issue from themselves, not from universal or Cosmic destiny.

Without Organic Cosmic Purpose, they function by reference to captive and arbitrary horizons of ethical inorganicism and the polarities of societal "good" or "bad."

Part 3

Realize that even as none can have beingness that is not organically related to the All-Presence, which consists of All of existence, also, can no one have a genuine purpose which is not harmoniously related to all the other righteous purposes inherent in existence in accord with The Creator's plan.

Beware of leading people who have lost their purpose – even more so, beware of being led by them! For of what direction and compass is knowledge unto a people who have lost their purpose?

Who can govern or educate their children on Cosmic Destiny, True-Will, and Purpose?

Beware how you listen to them! Listening to their Creator is the safest direct way to give ear unto all their misfortunes and woes. Listening to their Creator is the only path and source of hope and illumination unto their cause. You must become aware that listening to The Creator is listening to the Voice of more than everything in a people.

Where the people have lost their purpose, the easiest and shortest way of bridging the evolutionary chasm is by executing a successful revolution in listening to the Original Source and Cause of Destiny: their Creator, the One and Only Voice of Eternal and Omnipresent Reality of Salvation.

Our planet is on every side filled today with races, movements, organizations, cults, religions, education, technology, and politics – many of which have lost their worthy and truthful purposes. Nor would they rise to new higher ideals, nor would they let any others rise.

Billions are the captives of purposes, which were at some time in the evolutionary period of this plane useful, but which are today utterly inapplicable by reference to all the higher emergent conditions and new destinies which we call our times.

Many once-great races and religions today suffer and flounder, owing to unmanageable conditions of loss of purposes. The chaos that peoples and institutions which have lost their purposes exert upon our world testifies to the fact that many of our well-meaning group organs are leading the cause of highly inorganic and fabricated purposes – nor would they embrace new more workable ideals – nor would they let others do so. The inertia of their loss of purpose becomes a collective stagnation.

The loss of one's natural purposes makes one unable to acknowledge that there is a natural purpose in whatever else there may exist.

Chapter 4

Womanhood is Humanhood & More

The struggle for women's liberation must by its inherent nature be only fifty percent women's labor and the other half (50%) men's labor. For, in every woman and man, there is a man and woman – both of whom we must recognize, reconcile, and unify in love.

Individuals and societies cannot be free and harmonious until both the woman and man within each one is securely acknowledged and liberated. Women's suppression is men's oppression!

Genuine WOMANHOOD POWER, HONOR, and DUTY is a Cosmic TRUST!

What are men but women in handsome hoods embellished for the soul's earthly embodiment, and who are women but men in beautiful hoods, adorned for the soul's Cosmic evolvement; The hood is but the being's fleshly habiliment - a garment of life en route of mortal destiny.

Womanhood is Humanhood and Life!

Although the souls be hooded man and woman, the conscious being is the same within. Everyone, equally true of the man and for the woman, the ovum and the sperm are fused to create ALL. In The Creator's gift of character and splendor, he or she is neither more possessed of nor more beloved of destiny.

Womanhood is Humanhood and Soul!

To know the soul, their hoods all must prevail, and a happy surprise were all people to realize, If a woman or man: Asian, Mayan, African, and Aryan, the person of each hood elicits in every person working and unfolding a wondrous special aspect in the annals of common destiny.

Womanhood is Humanhood and Wisdom!

Consider thy self-same identity and difference; also consider the neuter nature of the soul. Man and woman shine in ALL women and men through and beyond their carnal hoods. The soul designs the carnal hood for the responsibility of liberating experience, which buoys and sails the wings of destiny.

Womanhood is Humanhood and Grandeur!

Yes, in one and the same, soulful individuality supremely resides a corporeal man and woman, polarized to a male and a female ministration, yet indivisibly embraced as a single inviolate entity; the sex is but a transient temporal formation that's essential to a transient physical destiny.

Womanhood is Humanhood and Power!

Humanity errs to thwart this balance in divinity, through the malefic ascendancy of manly egotism or in loitering by the bungle of antique traditions. At the same time, demeaning obstacles afflict goddess humanity, thereby appointing the fall of the very god himself contrary to their rising and mutual destiny.

Womanhood is Humanhood and Goddess!

Convene the nations by freedom, justice, and equality, for to liberate humankind through divine womanhood, may efforts in progress usher in love and wisdom, and mortals inspired beyond belly, racism, and sexism, renouncing every oppression to let women liberation follow the path of true destiny.

Womanhood is Humanhood and Future!

In all things, The Ever-present Creator of All is witness and judge supreme. Its motion and verdict are the highest possible perfection of justice. In the flux and process of universal and Cosmic organicism, in no spheres are any individuals lawfully commanded to give complicity to their own inquiry and undoing.

Pure love, as the substantive of co-operative and harmonious intelligence, in The Creator and Its creations, objectively binds persons together for their own good. And for their own good also, may The Creator unbind or separate them.

Womanhood is Humanhood and More!

Chapter 5

Highly Beloved and Most Darling

O' how can you confess her to be beloved and darling! If when she cries, "I am," you judge her offending and guilty: Is she truly beloved who you do not grant to say "I am."

True Love is commitment to the triumph of The Creator!

O' how can you confess her to be beloved and darling! If when she cries, "I know," you judge her offending and guilty: Is she truly beloved who you do not grant to say, "I know."

True Love is commitment to the triumph of Wisdom!

O' how can you confess her to be beloved and darling! If when she cries, "I will," you judge her offending and guilty: Is she truly beloved who you do not grant to say, "I will."

True Love is commitment to the triumph of Life!

O' how can you confess her to be beloved and darling! If when she cries, "I believe," you judge her offending and guilty: Is she truly beloved who you do not grant to say, "I believe."

True Love is commitment to the triumph of Loyalty!

O' how can you confess her to be beloved and darling! If when she cries, "I think," you judge her offending and guilty: Is she truly beloved who you do not grant to say, "I think."

True Love is commitment to the triumph of Truth!

O' how can you confess her to be beloved and darling! If when she cries, "I choose," you judge her offending and guilty: Is she truly beloved who you do not grant to say, "I choose."

True Love is commitment to the triumph of Freedom!

O' how can you confess her to be beloved and darling! If when she cries, "I hope," you judge her offending and guilty: Is she truly beloved who you do not grant to say, "I hope."

True Love is commitment to the triumph of Progress!

O' how can you confess her to be beloved and darling! If when she cries, "I belong," you judge her offending and guilty: Is she truly beloved who you do not grant to say, "I belong."

True Love is commitment to the triumph of Organicism!

O' how can you confess her to be beloved and darling! If when she cries, "I suffer," you judge her offending and guilty: Is she truly beloved who you do not grant to say, "I suffer."

True Love is commitment to the triumph of Peace!

O' how can you confess her to be beloved and darling! If when she cries, "I empower," you judge her offending and guilty: Is she truly beloved who you do not grant to say, "I empower."

True Love is commitment to the triumph of Creation!

O' how can you confess her to be beloved and darling! If when she cries, "I love," you judge her offending and guilty: Is she truly beloved who you do not grant to say, "I love."

True Love is commitment to the triumph of Perfection!

Chapter 6

~~~

Care is the Supreme Art

Every movement and exertion of the soul consists of an expression of will.

Self-will is motion by reference only to one's own concern.

Creator-Will works for the concern and good of All and represents direct Creator inspiration and proceedings throughout all of existence.

Creator-Will consists of the real Light and Law of the Omnipresent Whole.

Care is the key and art of practicing the true figure and ambience of Light as the perfection of love.

Careless life and use of mind expresses in the physical world as ill-will rather than as good-will.

Care is the grand-mother of all arts for making creature-will harmonious with Creator-Will.

Love: There are boundless opportunities for all who care to love and would care as devoutly as loving existence care commands. People of true care attend all with perfect heed, tenderness, and blessing, and empower all to a fuller expression of life and happiness.

Care is the art of recognizing love, and there's no finer art!

Sometimes an understanding silence and a gracious sentiment, pouring abroad a gift of love nursed in genuine performance, or maybe, a well-wishing so pure that it waters withering vines, be it ever fair weather or foul – real care is the soul's delight.

Care is the art of sharing love, and there's no worthier art!

We must ponder the nature of all things that touch life, in the seen and the unseen. What generates such sublime love than real care made manifest as the impetus for rendering love?! It is everlasting care that makes possible everlasting love.

Care is the art of creating love, and there's no greater art!

Now, behold the classic custom which folks have called love, for all the wealth and all the romances it does often boast, never was a person's love ever truer than the care is true, for love becomes a hoax where true care is hidden from folks.

Care is the art of enthroning love, and there's no loftier art!

Rejoice for the fortune if your care is alive and expressed, for by living care, life's universal law doth forever thrive. When inspired to care, souls, their greatest of love discover. But, without caring, none entertains real opportunity of love.

Care is the art of nurturing love, and there's no wiser art!

Care is the key to remembering, finding, and restoring love; it is the godly key for realizing beauty, justice, and truth; it is the key to lawful progress amidst uncheatable destiny; it is a dancing in the soul to the songs of inspiring Light.

Care is the art of balancing love, and there's no holier art!

Chapter 7

A Feeling of Belonging

With innumerable souls as its passengers and spangled with sub-systems of stars, suns, and planets, the mighty vortex of our local universe shuttles like a rocket through Etherea.

A feeling of belonging homes upon all, but to whom or where a person belongs?

No one's wisdom can tell you of limits. I see and feel not any limits whatsoever!

I know of no limits to where we all belong; our nativity is the Eternal and Cosmic.

Amidst mineral and vegetable kingdoms, there exists never a clue of their limit.

Within the spirit and animal worlds, one's effort is lost who seeks for limit.

There is no limit to where all belong or to whom and whence any person belongs.

In all the worlds and all the spheres, we belong, they belong, and ALL belong!

Me, I belong to ALL people as they like. I cherish the Cosmic for my true nativity, knowing my true home is in ALL the worlds. Here, I belong to each and to ALL alike.

I am their labor, and they are my service, and we ALL are one another's rewards!

Here, I was, I am, and I remain – IMMORTAL!

Look, I fancy not when I wasn't aware of being an immortal Being; I count NOTHING as a beginning and ending!

Though worlds may bid I live by boundary, I still can see without and far beyond. In vain, one seeks for limit in anything. In vain, one feels anything is peripheral. In vain, one thinks death limits belonging.

Never a limit to where I more or less abide. Nor limits both as the atom and as the Cosmos – for the Cosmic is charged upon ALL beings!

Yes, we are where limits exist - NOT AT ALL! Open are worlds, planes, and spheres of gods to come and go but never cease belonging! Traveling through Aquarius, by Afrika I go to enjoy the works and glory of creation.

As The Creator's children may travel material realms of God, as many travel Nirvana, Venus, and Mars, as many roam galaxies in missions of love, cruising as fast as the speed of thoughts and soon inhabit and migrate about stars, I belong to every star there might be.

Having Life and Will in the Omnipresent Will and never resting than The Creator retires.

Beyond how's and why's of forms and times, I am forever a citizen of the Cosmic!

I am ever belonging to life and activity – belonging to truth, knowledge, and beauty!

Although we move in ramparts of antiquity, is not progression our boundless destiny?!

Yes, I Am ETERNAL Cosmic part and belonging. Our ENTIRE Cosmos backs ALL individuality.

I live in ALL that's called your universes, nor have you any more world than my world. Dear Creator and creation BELONG together. Good-bye to any limits to endless belonging!

I wish NOT to belong to ANY LIMITS AT ALL: Cosmic Wholeness that's where ALL belong – and I neither know nor wish me otherwise!

Chapter 8

~~~~~

Cosmic Community for
Conscious Cosmic Citizenship

Being conscious of Cosmic citizenship is eternally the now-age ideal for harmonization, unification, and reconciliation with the truths of existence.

Every being is a citizen of the Cosmic first and foremost!

The Cosmic is the expansiveness and fullness of All there is as existence itself. It is infinite and eternal, and it constitutes the reality of the source of being and intelligence that is all-pervasive and permeates everyone and everything.

The Cosmic constitutes the very Presence of the Absolute. Everything and everyone have their being in It, by virtue of It, and is responsible for knowing It.

It is The IAM that we each are, with every breath we take, with each beat of our heart, and with Its intelligence, order, and law imprinted on every fiber of our Being.

We are not separate from our Creator. We dwell as points of Its Presence and dwelling. Consciously as points of Its Presence, in and by the Light of Its Presence, is that which will allow us to be reinstated, reoriented, and reconciled with the truth of ourselves, our purposes, duties, and responsibilities in being.

The institutions of the society in which we live have taken responsibility for educating us, orienting us towards nationalistic citizenship, which cannot take precedence over our Cosmic citizenship. Cosmic citizenship is our first point of reference in being.

We have been groomed to the tenants of capitalism, nationalism, patriotism, religions, and all manners of social association and group identifications, which lay the foundation for the tremendous issues we face as a nation. We are undermined by speciesism, racism, sexism, classism, bigotry, prejudice, homophobia, and all the other isms and schisms that erroneously justify the neglect, ill-treatment, hostility, oppression, lack of respect, honor, justice, and humanity that millions have and are continuing to experience at the hands of the government, religious, educational, medical communities, as well as individuals masquerading as so-called leaders.

Conscious Cosmic citizenship is prerequisite for being qualified for continuance in existence and escape the recurring wheel of incarnation into flesh. The dysfunction, degradation, and disease of individuals, families, communities, and nations of the world have endangered the rights of the peoples to be continued in existence.

As ALL are held accountable to the law, order, and the absolute and eternal governance of All existence: it is wisdom to heed the call to consciousness, commitment, and continuance by accepting one's immortal Reality and by applying oneself to the studies of Conscious Cosmic Citizenship.

Chapter 9

~~~

The Cosmic IAM Revelations
of The Creator of All

To the Glory of the Ever-present
Cosmic Supreme Being - THE COSMIC IAM

Part 1

1:1 - O'Ever-present Cosmic Supreme Being, I am an immortal part of you, and you are The Creator over All, in All, for All, with All, from All, unto All, about All, and throughout All.

1:2 - You are the Infinite and Eternal Cosmic Supreme Being and Creator over all individual intelligences, individual great spirits, individual great goddesses and gods, individual divinities and principalities, and individual great avatars, saviors, prophets, saints, and generals.

1:3 - You are the Supreme and Absolute Allness of Cosmic Reality.

1:4 - You are the inherent and succinct beginningless and endlessness of unmanifest Omnipresence. You are full capacity and the entire essence of Cosmic True Being.

1:5 - Your wheel, O' Ever Present Cosmic Supreme Being, is the primal motion by which, and towards which, all things are progressively driven in the fulfillment of your never-ending Cosmic designs and purpose.

1:6 - O' Boundless Ocean of Will, it is by your direct Presence and capacity as Cosmic Supreme Intelligence, and within your very living and boundless Body-Cosmic, that All creation is conceived, involved, evolved, revolved, convolved, and resolved.

1:7 - The diversity of your creation is an infinitude and you have made all things abundant in both reality and potentiality.

1:8 - O' Most Loving and Beloved, raise me to become truly and fully conscious as a Cosmic citizen: a living intelligent, loving, and potent part of you.

1:9 - Your capacity is everywhere present throughout the seen and the unseen. By your capacity, O' Boundless

One, all creation is upheld and unified within the perfect integrity of your Cosmic purposes and plans.

1:10 - You have created innumerable heavenly mother and father goddesses and gods, great spirits, intelligences, chieftains, divinities, elementals, angels, lords, and ladies, to organize, administer, and magnify your glory throughout your countless super-spiritual dimensions, corporeal worlds, grand-universes, systems, constellations, galaxies, and kingdoms.

1:11 - Your infinite Spirit is the soul of All and Everything. By your Infinite Light, the Spirit is formed, illuminated, and caused to be intelligent soul.

1:12 – You are the direct writer and revelator upon the souls of all things, of universal and Cosmic significances, values, and destinies.

1:13 - You are, O'Most Wonderful One, The Creator of our own beautiful local heavens and earth, and the suns and firmament local thereto.

1:14 - The powerful, wise, and high-raised heavenly father-mother gods and goddesses are your sons and daughters of superior accomplishments and superb organic progression in adept love, duty, and honor.

1:15 - You have placed them before humans and ex-humans as examples of heights attainable by all who abide devoutly in the Light and Love of thy Will and service.

1:16 - Is not to raise humans and ex-humans to goddesses and gods, O'Ever-present Cosmic Supreme Being, the labor of thy Light, the blessing of the earth, and the destiny of both the higher and lower heavens?!

1:17 - O'Ever-present, to truly discover you is to become conscious of my own true Being, identity, power, and purpose. To call unto you is to call upon my own soul, upon all your creatures throughout infinite creation, and upon All the Cosmic for support and love. To love you truly is to serve everyone and All things.

1:18 - O'Ever-present Cosmic Supreme Being, you are the very Infinity and Eternity and Totality of manifested and unmanifested reality.

1:19 - You are the Boundless Ocean of Cosmic Will, and capacity within which resides and flows Cosmic Intelligence, Cosmic Power, Cosmic Law, Cosmic Life, Cosmic Spirit, Cosmic Matter, Cosmic Energy, Cosmic Labor, Cosmic Light, and Cosmic Love.

1:20 - You are the Supreme and Absolute Being of all Beings, seen and unseen, by humans or by angels, and by gods and goddesses.

1:21 - You are absolutely the Presence of all presence, the Substance of all essence, the Life of all life, the Intelligence of all intelligences, the Purpose of all purposes, the Love of all love, the Joy of all bliss, and the Ultimate Parent-Reality of all fathers and mothers.

1:22 - O'Thou Infinite and Loving Verity, you are All and Everything! Surely, you are the absolute and indivisible unity of Cosmic reality, diversified within Its own inalienable integrity of eternal wholeness and oneness.

1:23 - In both Cosmic and local omnipresence, you are Perfect, Ultimate, and Absolutely Supreme. In duration, you are both all times and timeless eternity.

1:24 - Certainly, you are beyond all qualifications and degrees or any names that any beings might choose to call you. Indeed, no one other than you, yourself, spans your Cosmic infinitude to comprehend it All.

1:25 - You are the Ultimate Reality of non-ultimate beings, and you are the only Ultimate Being there is and that there will ever be.

1:26 - You are Creator within and over all considerations, forms, ambiences, units, substances, categories, and significances.

1:27 - O'Ever-present Cosmic Supreme Being, it is marvelous and wonderful that we are all inseparable and imperishable parts of you.

1:28 - To call upon your support is to call upon everyone and upon All things throughout All of existence.

Part 2

2:1 - O'Ever-present Cosmic All-Person, your direct Cosmic parenthood is the very womb in which all beings and things are conceived, and from which nothing can be delivered.

2:2 - You are All at once, the Cosmic crucible, and smith of all forms, and ambiences of spiritual, corporeal, and unmanifested creation.

2:3 - Your direct Presence is both all things and the capacity that upholds all things. Within your administration of adversary judgments over all the innumerable visible and invisible, corporeal, and spiritual-super-universes, galaxies, and worlds you are Creator – and they are all living and moving parts of your substantive Presence. You are their immediate and Ultimate Parent-Reality forever.

2:4 - Yes, you are The Creator in the smallest of the smallest, in the greatest and the loftiest, in the right and the wrong, and You are forever blessing and upholding All in thy essence, will, and love.

2:5 - Certainly, all Beings and things are points in and of the direct Presence of your Omnipresent Body-Cosmic.

2:6 - You are Creator over all local and heavenly fathers and mothers of all living things, including all gods and goddesses, saints and saviors, gurus and avatars, the knowing-ones, plants, animals, minerals, and diverse orders and sublimities of spirit.

2:7 - Throughout all heavens and all worlds, no matter what their harmony or chaos may be, you are the Ultimate Parent of All of creation. Yes, you are Creator and Father-Mother of the presiding goddesses and gods of our own local earth and heavens and their local systems and firmaments.

2:8 - O'All Encompassing and Wondrous Womb, am I not perpetually, and ever sustained, nourished, renewed, and reborn in you – and you in me?!

2:9 - O'Cosmic IAM, am I not of, in, and ever with, that, that you are?!

2:10 - O'Ever-present Cosmic Great Spirit, you are Creator of and over all individual great spirits and souls.

2:11 - Spirit is only the soul of things in Your Cosmic Reality; but you are everything. Your immeasurable reality is in totality unnamable by any finite class or genders, and for that reason has been called Infinite and Eternal by the wisdom of your Presence in folks and gods.

2:12 - Yes, you are both Creator and embodiment of all and every unit state, form, function, ideal, and category of creation or consciousness, and you are all consciousness comprehending.

2:13 - Sure, it is your direct Presence which capacitates and configurates itself as diverse states of consciousness in order to meet the requirements of thy purposes, harmony, and love.

2:14 - Your Presence is the true alchemy, essence, vitality, and substance of all beings, and of all things.

2:15 - O'Being of beings, no one can be without being in every way a part of your Being.

2:16 - All at once, your substantive Presence is the very matter, mind, essence, capacity, intellect, power, process, performance, love, ethic, and integrity of every entity.

2:17 - Your Presence is the eternal abidance that is in eternal progression.

2:18 - The distortion of thy Presence and Light is the sorrow of creatures. The so-called *evil* is only due to creation distorting the harmony of the Light of your direct Presence – and there is no evil otherwise.

2:19 - Your Presence is my own very presence and to worship you is to witness to your Presence in my own soul, everyone, and all things.

2:20 - To embrace you, must not my own Being extend with love through all things, all places, and all conditions?!

Part 3

3:1 - O'Ever-present Supreme IAM, you are the Macro IAM of all micro IAM.

3:2 - You are beyond all highs and heights, and Creator over all glory and exaltedness.

3:3 - Humanity is not only your glory, but you have granted it the destiny of multiplying and magnifying your glory.

3:4 - The intelligences of grand-universes and superlative inter-dimensional and intergalactic systems; the goddesses and the gods of Nirvana, and of the lower heavens and earth, are all your manifest glory for the magnification of thy created glory!

3:5 - Yes, you are Creator in and over all triune-beings, lords, lord-gods, goddesses, avatars, masters, gurus, saviors, prophets, saints, adepts, generals, and their multitudes.

3:6 - Yes, all resident humans and ex-humans of earth involuntarily represent thy Presence, or otherwise, denying the same.

3:7 - By the distortion of the Light of thy Presence, chaos and inharmony as the "devil" are acted out by elements of free will in creation. Your organic reality is without inherent devil or evil.

3:8 - O'Ever-present IAM, to perform in your Illumination is to live perfectly and at one with All things!

3:9 - You are, O'Ever-present Boundlessness, the Eternal Wholeness and unity that is beyond phenomenal diversity and aggregation.

3:10 - You are the Infinitude that is Absolute and All-Inclusive, beyond and above all arbitrariness, all thoughts, all postulates, all ideals, all dimensions, all coordinates, measurements, and all genders, known and unknown in the microcosm.

3:11 - It is your dynamic and abiding Presence which grants all consciousness, all abilities, all grounds, all motion, all purposes, and all significances to all entities and identities in creation. It is your Presence which allots true responsibilities, consciousness, and enlightened self-expression that they might choose to pursue.

3:12 - You are the Supreme and Cosmic administrator and counselor within All, throughout All, and over All.

3:13 - You are looking at the world through the eyes of the smallest insect and through the vortices of the grandest universes.

3:14 - You are the giver of All and the receiver of All, and the Most Loving and Beloved. Indeed no one can serve you without you or offend you without you – neither can anyone love you without you!

3:15 - All things, without any exceptions, happen or fail to happen within your Infinite, Eternal, Living, and All-Intelligent Body-Cosmic.

3:16 - O'All Love and Supreme Wisdom, how great and joyful I feel knowing I am an immortal child of yours and knowing that the children of The Creator are surely destined to become real goddesses and gods.

3:17 - What best ways are there to speak of the highest truth than to speak of thee; to apply to the highest love than to apply to thee; to seek power and potency than to seek in thee.

3:18 - O'Ever-present Veracity of Cosmic Reality, your Presence is the highest and lowest common denominator of all beings' ideas, conditions, and significances. Your Presence is the substance of the tangible, subtle, and unmanifested.

3:19 - O'Cosmic Supreme Being; O'Light and Life of all microcosm, is not all consciousness the mode of flow of the essence and capacity of thy direct Presence, proceeding and progressing towards thy purposes?!

3:20 - O'Cosmic IAM, is it not thy Will to motion power, love, wisdom, thrill, form, and beauty, which is called consciousness?!

3:21 - O'Most Instant and Beneficent counselor of All, you are the Supreme Knowledge and Absolute knower.

3:22 - No beings, no matter what their order may be, can add one iota of intelligence and substance to their stature, form, or worth, without taking from thee and giving the same unto thee.

3:23 - You are the True-Self of all selves. There is no god or goddess, or any great spirit and intelligence, or any human or ex-human, or any character of elements, or any material or subtle worlds, anywhere, which stand upon their own grounds, breathe their own elements, float within their own atmosphere and essence apart from that which derives from the reality of thy direct Presence.

3:24 - You are the common ground of All reality and all possibilities. You are capacitor, the upholder, and the upheld.

3:25 - All so-called co-creators are mere parts of your own Cosmic Entity under your impetus and command – neither can they produce any elements that were not already in existence as part of thee.

3:26 - You are the circle without periphery and the cycle without ending.

3:27 - O'Thou Beginningless and Endlessness, you are the All-Central, and I thrill in the realization that I am an immortal and inalienable part of you, and that you are the Eternal and Boundless Whole of me.

Part 4

4:1 - O'Everywhere Present Supreme Cosmic Reality, I am a part of your Living, and you are the Whole of my living; I am a part of your Intelligence, and you are the Whole of my intelligence; I am a part of your Consciousness, and you are the Whole of my consciousness; I am a part of your Labor, and you are the Whole of my labor; I am a part of your Capacity, and you are Whole of my capacity; I am a part of your Spirit, and you are the Whole of my spirit; I am part of your Substances, and you are the Whole of my substances; I am a part of your Proceedings, and you are the Whole of my proceedings: I rely upon the Whole of you, and you rely upon the part of you that I am. Are we not together Absolutely one as the Infinite and Eternal Cosmic IAM?!

4:2 - O' Light of my life, is not all progress the march of your creation from one applicable and accomplished destiny unto others?!

4:3 - The waters, the earth, the air, and the fire elements are corporeal qualities of the substance of your direct Presence. You have formed them in the construction of our local stars, sun, moons, worlds, and their residents - you have breathed your Dynamic Spirit into their forms to elicit living souls in them.

4:4 - Yes, your Presence is both spirit and the manifest physical and the unmanifested; it is light and shade, night and day, and sound and silence.

4:5 - Color, thoughts, faith, conscience, research, reason, desire, feeling rejoiceful, order, attention, beauty, power, freedom, and spontaneous awareness are all acts of thy Will within the capacity of thy conscious Light.

4:6 - Within your all-knowing and all-thinking and all-doing Self, you have created and made each and every individual human being heir to both our male and female Cosmic faculties and all the glories attendant thereunto.

4:7 - From one life and world unto endless life and worlds of eternal progression – through the worlds of being human unto heavens of being ex-humans – defying the portals of death and emerging past ethereal planets and planes, visible and invisible – you are the rule, the ruler, and ruled, all by your own direct Presence.

4:8 - Your limitations are the limitations in the nature of your developing creations. Faults are the faults of creations distorted light of intelligence and abused imagination.

4:9 - All beings participate as elements of your Cosmic Reality and proceedings.

4:10 - O'Thou Creator of All, to know you is to know everything truly. But the distortion of the Light of your Presence, by your creations, is sorrow, illusion, and the very "devil."

4:11 - Thou art that absolute Cosmic administrator and Supreme counselor, and every order, hierarchy, and government of the seen and the unseen, of the animate and the inanimate, and of the mobile and stationary, is directly within your Cosmic administration.

4:12 - You are the land and its people, and the heavens and their spirits, and your ways of progress are the same for all things and beings.

4:13 - A corporeal particle of creation, existing in your Light, is far more joyful than a heavenly god or goddess in darkness.

4:14 - The abuse of your Presence in things, as things in places and in times, O'Creator in and over All, is the very meaning of chaos and hell; but is not the love and practice of your Presence real peace and harmony?!

4:15 - Are not your creatures desiring you with your own desires, looking for you with your own very eyes, and forgetting that the children of The Creator can only be goddesses and gods and should model their lives accordingly?!

4:16 - O'Most Harmonious and Most Beloving Governance of All, is not true independence conscious dependence upon thy Omnipresent Will?! Is not true individuality being consciously aware of oneness with thy Infinite Spirit of Love and Light?!

Part 5

5:1 - Everyone, no matter what may be the system or order to which they belong, no matter whether or not they accept a name for thee, or whether they worship idols made of thy matter, or otherwise chosen from amidst thy innumerable and diverse ranks of heavenly entities: gods, goddesses, lords, builders, gurus, and ex-ambassadors of certain worlds, practice thy light each moment they live by their highest applicable truth.

5:2 - Truth, O'All Veracity, is the highest applicable knowing concerning your Presence and its inherent conjunctions and proceedings.

5:3 - To honor you is to truly honor my soul, everyone, and all things all at once!

5:4 - Is not the worship, magnification, and acknowledgment of the Whole the only salvation from idolatry?!

5:5 - By your Life and Light, all thoughts are formed, and all minds organized – neither can anyone's ideals and ideas cause any original things to come into existence.

5:6 - Human thinking is merely holding the Light of thy Creative Intelligence upon creation.

5:7 - Do not entities use, or otherwise, abuse, thy direct Presence, calling the use *good* and the abuse *evil* - although your Presence is only Love and the Way?!

5:8 - You have put your thoughts upon free-floating corporeal substance and produced material physical states and forms, worlds, stars, atoms, and universes, and by your direct presence you have sustained their motives.

5:9 - O'Boundless Boundary of all bounds, O'All One, you are the Positive and Supreme monitor of all levels of diversity.

5:10 - You forever transcend and encompass all good or bad, up or down, yin or yang, saint or devil, male or female, right or wrong, and true or false. Is not "duality" for the souls who hesitate to rise above two-in-one to perceive infinity and eternity of diversity in the one?!

5:11 – What, O'Absolute Wholeness, is duality but the passing conjecture in the fixation of your imagining and thinking entities of creation, concerning the working of your events, cycles, products, and conjunctions, by reference to their own illusions and separate desires and will?!

5:12 - Surely, you are Infinite and Eternal Unity without divisions, vacancy, vacuum, or any chasm, demarcation, zeros, sects, sexes, likes or dislikes, and or any emptiness.

5:13 - Cosmic is the perfect integrity of the fullness and unity of your direct personal Presence as Infinity and Eternity of Absolute and Supreme Being.

5:14 - Your Supreme Presence, as Infinity and Eternity of Absolute and Supreme Being, is without duality, religion, color, and ideology, for or against any parts of elements of itself. All parts of thy Supreme Being are charged alike in the Breath and Light of thy Omnipresence Reality.

5:15 - To see, rise, and express your undistorted Light is your uniform Plan, Prayer, Will, and Command for all orders of creation.

5:16 - Your very person is the undistorted Life and Light, and your Harmony is upon the universes and the atom.

5:17 - To those who seek and rise to conscious affiliation, responsibility, and honor in the expression of love in thy Body-Cosmic, You have graciously capacitated to the ever-exulting level of Cosmic citizenship, conscious evolutionary development and progression, conscious immortality, and conscious daughterhood and sonship, or goddesshood and godhood.

5:18 - O'Substance of all selves, your Presence is All things linked and unified, apart and together – it is the gathering integrity of all entities and forms within formless Omnipresence of your Being and capacity.

5:19 - O'Ever-present, you are the One Truth that Totally, Absolutely, and Purposefully aligns, regulates, harmonizes, embodies, and unifies All truths.

5:20 - O'All Truth, all diversity is within your indissoluble Cosmic Unity and Integrity. Certainly, you are the Fullness of all the power, substance, and potency there is and that there will ever be.

5:21 - You have foreseen all the future because you are all the future there will ever be. You know all of the past because you are all the past there was ever; the fullness of all the present is the now-currency of your Cosmic Omnipresence.

5:22 - In your Body-Cosmic, and its worlds-beyond numbers, O'Most Loving and Beloved, you have provided just and orderly ways and means of progressive evolutionary qualification for eternally grading, posting, honoring, and elevating your created souls, from one plane of conscious adeptism and sublimity to endless other planes.

5:23 - Your infinite Cosmic cycles have set the tone for the eternal procession and progression of your Reality.

5:24 - You are personally the music and the dance, the player and the spectator, the believer and the unbeliever, the passive and the active, the theist and the atheist, the illuminated and the occluded, the servant and the served.

5:25 - For those who choose the path of your conscious Light, your ways are of Boundless Abundance – and there is nothing you have made scarce in reality or in possibility.

5:26 - Your Cosmic Womb is forever caressing, convolving, and flowing with common creation, or with undiscovered old and new creation.

5:27 - Under the Light of your Supreme Intelligence, O'Cosmic Being of beings, your children travel through endless worlds, universes, super-universes, and grand-dimensions, from discoveries unto discoveries, or from one life unto numberless other lives of eternal progression.

5:28 - O'Most Unfathomable One, your marvels and wonders, are at times, so unbelievable to both humans and ex-humans that angels and folks have called certain conditions of your presence "illusion." Nevertheless, real illusion does never exist beyond the shortcomings of human faculties – and all the so-called illusion is woven out of the fabric of your direct Presence, in and as substantive and inherent Reality.

5:29 - You are the Only All-Inclusive Reality and the Original Impetus of Power, Wisdom, and Love that will enable humans to the realization that they are the children of The Creator of goddesses and gods and that they are themselves destined to someday become conscious and mature goddesses and gods.

5:30 - Throughout the Cosmic, you are the Absolute Supreme Being and Ever-Present counselor, who forever teaches all beings how to attend one another with your Blessing and Love.

5:31 - In form, creations actions and significances, and for the good of All, O'Ever-present Cosmic Supreme

Being, thy Will, Power, Wisdom, Freedom, Beauty, Joy, Labor, Light, and Love be forever done!

To the Glory of the Ever-present Cosmic Supreme Being, The Creator of All that is All!

Chapter 10

Cosmic IAM Meditation System

1. Claim the entire presence of existence is of, and one with The Creator of All. Decree that the whole of all of presence and existence is The Creator of All that is All

2. Claim and or submit that you are an immortal point and a part of The Creator of All

3. Claim the Light of All of existence by calling for the presence of the Light of All of existence and by calling on The Creator's direct Presence

4. Recognize the attention of The Creator and submit for the attention of The Creator to be with you. You are to be mindful, attentive, worshipful, and obedient to be with It

5. Decree peace for All of existence – claim and decree peace for your own direct presence, soul, and Being

6. Meditate in the attention of The Creator, and submit for The Creator of All to guide you to attain True Organic Reality

7. Proclaim and surrender to The Creator that you be at truth. Truth is the position and the decision of The Creator, for and towards all and everything, and or concerning The Creator's own Will on any matter

8. Meditate on being conscious of your immortal Beingness and meditate on being conscious of being within The Creator's Presence

9. Meditate on being conscious of the feeling of The Creator in existence and meditate on being conscious of the feeling of your own immortal Being

10. Meditate on feeling and the Light of The Creator being adjusted harmoniously together – that your knowing and feeling be taught by The Creator of All, about The Creator

11. Meditate on being one with The Creator of All with conscious mindfulness, attention, worship, and obedience

12. Meditate on the unison of The Creator of All direct. Making sure that you are with the Light in feeling

13. Meditate in The Creator of All, appealing and submitting for The Creator to meditate in you. That The Creator's Presence be in meditation and attention for you, in you, and towards you

14. Meditate in The Creator of All that you are conscious of It with your whole presence and Being

15. Direct your meditation viewpoint in the direction of the unqualified/unmanifest Presence of The Creator

16. Obey The Creator of All, unqualifiedly, while in the meditation, and afterward

17. Cosmic meditation is the perfection of communication by The Creator with Its creation, and the creation must be mindful, attentive, worshipful, and obedient to remain with perfection of communication

In Summary:

- You are to claim and decree that you are a point and part of The Creator of All. The Creator being All there is as Presence and All the Presence there is

- You are then to meditate until you are visible to yourself in the presence of the whole, within which you are meditating

- After and upon seeing yourself perfectly, you are to decree all evils to dissolve and to void from you

- Then you are to concentrate your meditation until you behold The Creator of All - that you are at and with Its Presence, direct

- Once you behold The Creator, you should solemnly ask The Creator of All to assist you to reject, renounce, dissolve, and void all evil in yourself

- After you have submitted and allowed the dissolving of all ruses and or evil, you can meditate in peace and continue your concentration of meditation on listening to the communication and exchange of wisdom of The Creator of All

- Focusing and centering with The Creator of All should be for obtaining care, mindfulness, attention, communication, worship, obedience, peace, and holiness all at once. As to focus all those qualities into your point of union with The Creator of All

The Song of Destiny

This is a song Son would sing as celebration of the accomplishment of Destiny – the knowing and doing of The Creator's Will for one's point and part in the Cosmic plan:

"Now we sing like birds in the wilderness...
Birds in the wilderness...
Birds in the wilderness…
Now we sing like birds in the wilderness
'Cause we've done our part."

Contact:

Instagram @gold.encompass & @anthonyatonement

Twitter @Gold_Encompass

Gold-encompass.com

Made in the USA
Monee, IL
24 May 2022

96862508R10046